Introduction

This book shows the current range of 𝔒𝔯𝔠𝔥𝔞𝔯𝔡 𝔓𝔯𝔬𝔡𝔲𝔠𝔱𝔰 cake decorating tools and gives detailed instructions on how to make the best of their ease of use and versatility. All the items described are made using only the one set of cutters R1 — R14, a sharp pointed knife and the Petal-Shaped Box.
There is a video tape (VHS) available, which complements this book.

The Tools

General Notes.

Non-Stick.	One of the most useful aspects of their design is their non-stick property which is inherent in the material used. It is not a surface finish and, therefore, cannot wear off.
Materials.	All the tools can be used with any soft material such as flowerpaste, sugarpaste, marzipan, modelling chocolate, plasticine, modelling clay etc.
Temperature.	They will withstand boiling water or the dishwasher without deforming.
Handles.	All the cutters have comfortably sized hollow handles which allow you to exert firm pressure over the whole of the cutting edges.
Stability.	They will not rust, corrode, deform or wear out with normal useage.
Marking.	All the tools are clearly and permanently marked to aid easy identification, and are packed in appropriate containers or bags.
Metal.	They should not be brought into contact with sharp metal objects which may damage the cutting edges or surfaces, i.e. keep them separated from metal cutters.
Storage of Boards	Keep them in a cool dry place and, if storing several boards together, make sure they are quite dry before packing and, preferably, stand them on edge to allow air to circulate.
Hygiene.	The materials meet the appropriate EEC Regulations for food hygiene.
Endorsement.	All the items are personally endorsed and used by Pat Ashby, our Technical Director.

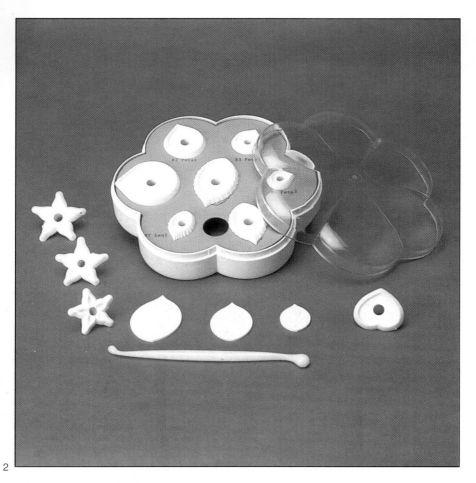

2

Ref. 1: The Rose Set. (10 items R1 — R10)

This comprehensive set combines 4 Petal Cutters, 3 realistically shaped Leaf Cutters, and 3 delicately veined Leaf Moulds (or veiners), all in an attractive petal-shaped box 6½″dia. (165mm), which itself is a very useful tool. The actual cut-out shapes are shown full size on Page 3. (Illustration 3).

Ref. 4: The Calyx and Briar Rose Petal Cutter Set. (R11, R12, R13, R14).

As you can see from Illustration 3 the Calyx cutters all come to fine points very like the real thing. The Briar Rose shape was taken from an actual petal. They form an ideal extension to the Rose Set enabling wired roses to be made and various other types of flower.

Ref. 28: The Balling Tool (OP1). Size — 5¼″ (133mm) long. The balling tool

has smoothly finished ends, is beautifully balanced and, like all other **Orchard Products** tools, does not stick.

The **ROSE SET** shapes (actual size)

Petal Cutters

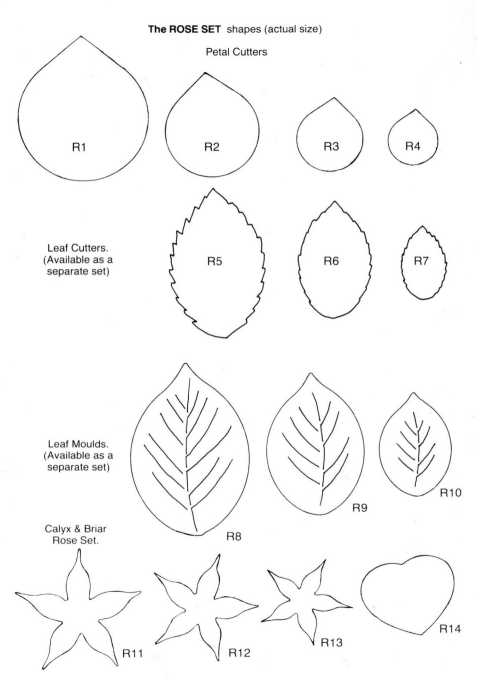

Leaf Cutters.
(Available as a
separate set)

Leaf Moulds.
(Available as a
separate set)

Calyx & Briar
Rose Set.

Illustration 3.

Non-Stick BOARDS and ROLLING PINS. *(See Illustrations 4 & 5)*

Ref. 20: 12" Board. Size - 12" × 9½" × ½" (300×240×12mm) with rubber feet
Ref. 21: 24" Board. Size - 24" × 19" × ½" (600×480×12mm) with rubber feet
Ref. 22: 10" Board. Size - 10" × 6¾" × ½" (250×170×12mm) with rubber feet

Ref. 25: 9" Rolling Pin. Size - 9" long × 1" dia. (230×25mm)
Ref. 26: 15" Rolling Pin. Size - 15" long × 1¾" dia. (380×44mm)
Ref. 27: 20" Rolling Pin. Size - 19½" long × 1¾" dia. (500×44mm)

These tools are made from a special plastic material which is a considerable advance on other more traditional materials such as marble or ordinary plastic surfaces — the 10" board and 9" pin being ideal for flower work, requiring little or no dusting, and slip easily into your workbox.
The rubber feet are essential to prevent the board from sliding.
The feet are drilled into the material and not just stuck on.
The 12" board is useful for flowers, plaques or other larger items and can easily be carried by students.
The 24" board and larger pins are very suitable for covering cakes (or making plaques) up to 12" dia. with marzipan or sugarpaste, again requiring little or no dusting with cornflour, sugar or fat. 'Polishing', therefore, is not normally required.**NB:** If a large amount of cutting with a sharp knife is to be done it is better to use just one corner for the purpose or turn the board over, since it may mark. If you turn it over use a damp cloth or Blu-Tack underneath to stop the board from slipping.
If the board does become badly marked it can probably be resurfaced for a small fee plus postage.

We can supply boards and pins of any reasonable size — to fit your worktop space? Please ask for a quotation giving actual size required.

Miscellaneous

Ref. 92: Book Stand (in clear plastic). Size — 8½" high x 12" wide × 3" deep (215×300×76mm). *(See illustration 6)*.
Ideal for reading an instruction book as you work, keeping the book clean and only taking up 3" of your work space.

Ref. 95: Book — 'FLOWERS AND OTHER IDEAS (the easy way)', in full colour, A5 size 32 pages. Detailed instructions on using 𝕺𝖗𝖈𝖍𝖆𝖗𝖉 𝕻𝖗𝖔𝖉𝖚𝖈𝖙 tools.

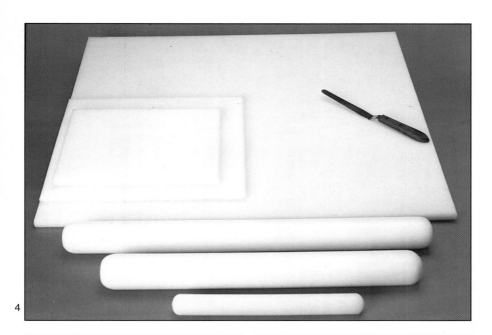

4

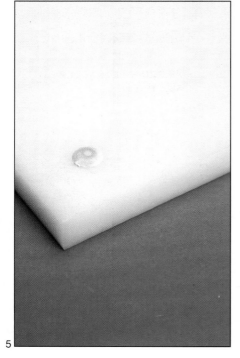

5

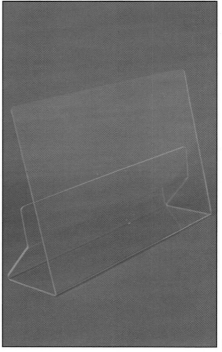

6

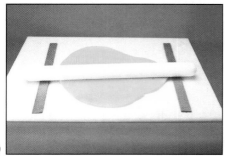

Using the Cutters. *(See Illustration 7)*

Roll out the paste very thinly (you should be able to see through it). The cutters have been designed to take a maximum thickness of $^3/_{32}$" (2mm). If the paste is too thick the hole in the handle will mark the paste.

Holding the cutter by its handle press firmly down onto the paste and then lift. There should be no need to rotate the cutter. The cut-out shape will remain on the board. (If the paste should stick in the cutter a light push with a blunt ended tool through the handle will quickly release it).

Notice how comfortable the handle is to hold, which means you can use the cutters for long periods without getting sore fingers.

When using flowerpaste, keep the paste covered with the lid of your box or a sheet of thick plastic while not actually cutting, to prevent drying out too soon.

Using the Leaf Moulds. *(See Illustration 8)*

Having cut out the leaf shape, turn the leaf over (with your cranked spatula) and place it in the centre of the appropriate size dusted leaf mould (R5 with R8, R6 with R9, R7 with R10).

You can, of course, vary this for special effects.

The mould is larger than the leaf thus allowing you to centre the leaf accurately. Dust the heel of your hand and press gently down on the leaf. Then remove the leaf. Curl as required and leave to dry on a piece of sponge.

Using the Non-Stick Boards and Rolling Pins.
These normally only require a very light dusting with cornflour (for flowerpaste) or caster or icing sugar (for marzipan), but can be used without any surface preparation. Fat oriented pastes may benefit from using a trace of fat on the surface.
A baby's nappy liner tied up into a bag with a small piece of wire makes an ideal dusting bag, giving just the required amount for these boards.
Because of the light dusting, premature drying out is avoided and 'polishing' is not normally necessary.
With marzipan, the elimination of loose sugar means that the pieces of marzipan will stick to each other easily without 'glue'
Roll out the material, working from the centre, until it is of the required thickness. There is no need to keep lifting it with the spatula or turning it. It will come away from the board quite easily.

Spacers. To give a uniform thickness easily with plaques or similar larger areas, use one of the larger rolling pins with long 'spacers' of the required thickness under each end of the pin — see illustration 9.

Cleaning. A wipe with a damp cloth is all that is normally required. Some colourings may stain the surface, but most proprietary non-abrasive cleaners or even toothpaste will remove unwanted marks. If all else fails a cleaner called 'Astonish' will do the trick. This is available from:-
    Emm & Bee (Leeds) Supplies
    Meanwood Road
    Leeds LS7 2JL   Tel: 0532 625206

How to Colour the Flowerpaste. (Recipe Page 31)
1. Cut a piece of paste and dip a cocktail stick into a **paste** colour. (Use paste colours since liquid colours tend to alter the consistency and drying properties of the flowerpaste).
    Add the cocktail stick of colour to the flowerpaste and knead thoroughly. Keep adding a **little** of the colouring at a time and mix thoroughly until the desired shade is obtained.
    If you are making several flowers of the same colour, colour enough flowerpaste for all of them at the same time to ensure a correct match. Always keep the paste you are not working on tightly wrapped or under a glass container to prevent drying out.
2. Alternatively the flowerpaste can be left white and the finished flower dusted with petal dust using a soft brush.

10

How to Make the Large Open Rose. *(See Illustration 10)*

1. Petals. Roll out the coloured paste very thinly — until you can see through it — and then cut out 6 large petals (R1), 5 medium petals (R2), 4 petals (R3) and 3 small petals (R4) for each flower. Cut out small batches at a time.

   Dust your hand with cornflour and pick up one petal with your angled spatula, covering the remaining petals with plastic or the lid of your box. Place the petal on your hand and smooth and frill out the edge all the way round with the balling tool (OP1) keeping the end of the tool half on the petal and half on your hand. (See illustration 11). Practice makes perfect!

   Put the petal onto a piece of dusted thick soft foam rubber and cup by pressing gently in the centre with a blunt tool such as the end of the rolling pin. (See illustration 12).

   For the larger petals, after balling the edge turn the petal over as you place it on the sponge. Then cup as above.

   If a sharper curl is required bend the edges back over a cocktail stick. (See illustration 13). Remove cocktail stick. Leave to dry, preferably overnight.

   Continue in the same way with the remaining petals using appropriately sized smooth blunt tools to cup the different sizes of petal, i.e. the smoothed end of a wooden spoon.

   The balling tool suits the R4 petal.

2. Leaves. Using green coloured flowerpaste, roll out thinly and cut 3 or 4 leaves for each flower. Vein the leaves with leaf moulds as on Page 6, curl and leave to dry.

3. Assembly. Take a square of waxed paper [approx. 3″ (75mm)] and cut diagonally towards the centre from each corner. (See illustration 14). Pipe a circle of stiff Royal Icing [about 1″ dia. (25mm)] on the shiny side using about a No. 4 size hole cut in the end of the icing bag. Place the heel of a large petal (R1) onto the circle. Repeat with the remaining 5 — R1 petals overlapping each one and tucking the last one under the first.

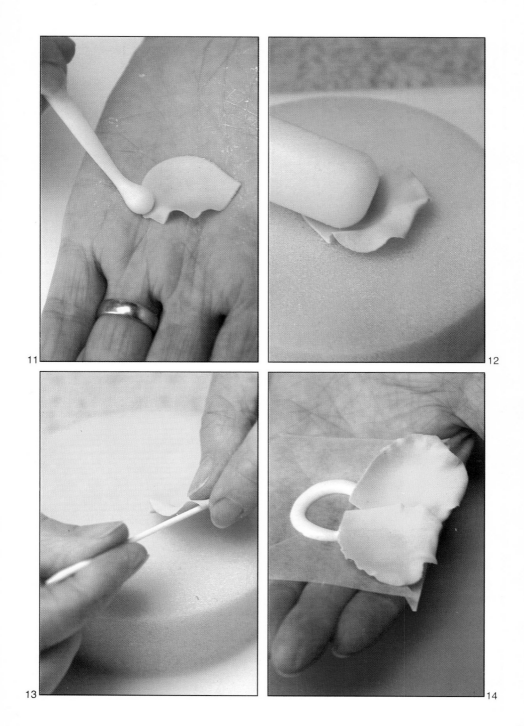

15

Adjust so that they form a more or less even circle. (See illustration 15).
Then pipe another circle of Royal Icing on top of the heels of the R1
petals. Place the 5 — R2 petals in the same way on top of the R1 petals,
starting with the centre of the first one over the join of two R1 petals. (See
illustration 16).

Pipe another circle of icing and repeat with R3 petals, and, if required,
with the R4 petals in the same way.

Place a little Royal Icing in the centre of the flower and cut about 5 or 7
stamens of slightly different lengths. Place the stamens in the centre with
tweezers. (See illustration 17).

Place the complete flower in an apple tray or shaped foil and finally
adjust the petals wider apart or closer as required. Leave to dry.

When dry, if required, dust the centre and/or edges of the petals with a
matching or contrasting colour petal dust.

4. Colouring Leaves. When the leaves are dry, dust the veined side with
petal dust using a soft wide brush. Brown and darker green are suitable
colours with perhaps a touch of red.
The leaves may be glazed with a confectioners glaze or Gum Arabic
glaze for greater realism. (See recipe Page 31).

5. Positioning the Flower. When the flower is dry peel off the waxed paper
and place a little Royal Icing on the cake or board and position the flower.
Put a spot of icing on the base of each leaf and position under the flower
as required.

How to Make the Small Open Rose. *(See Illustration 18)*

1. Proceed as for the large Open Rose but omit the largest petals (R1).

18

17

16

19

How to Make the Briar Rose. *(See Illustration 19)*

1. Make the centre first with a small ball of yellow paste and mark the surface by pressing firmly against a piece of tulle. (See illustration 20). Insert a large number of stamens, in multiples of five, of varying lengths with the longer curved ones on the outside and leaving a bare patch in the centre. Leave to dry. Highlight each stamen with yellow petal dust and a touch of brown paste colour.
2. Roll out a little green and white flowerpaste very thinly, place the two pieces on top of each other and roll again. (See illustration 21). Cut out a large calyx (R13). Cup the sepals slightly with the balling tool. (See illustration 22). Place in a greased plastic apple tray.
3. Roll out white paste very thinly and cut out 5 petals with the Briar Rose petal cutter (R14). Thin the edges with the balling tool but do not frill. Place them on thick dusted sponge and cup with a blunt tool. (See illustration 23).
4. Paint a touch of rose water, egg white or Gum Arabic glue in the centre of the calyx and along two adjoining sepals. Place the point of a petal to the centre of the calyx with the edge of the petal in line with the edge of the sepal. (See illustration 24). Using the glue continue placing the remaining petals in the calyx overlapping each one, with the last overlapping the first.
5. Paint a little glue in the centre of the petals and attach the centre of the flower (from Step 1). If required curl back the edges of some of the petals over a cocktail stick. Leave to dry.
6. When dry, petal dust the base of each petal with yellow, and then touch the edges with pink.

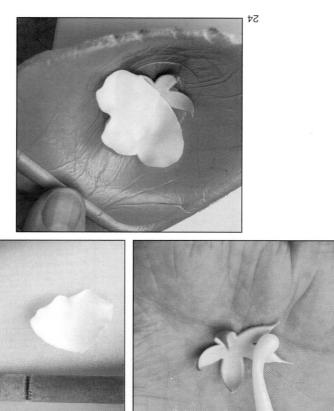

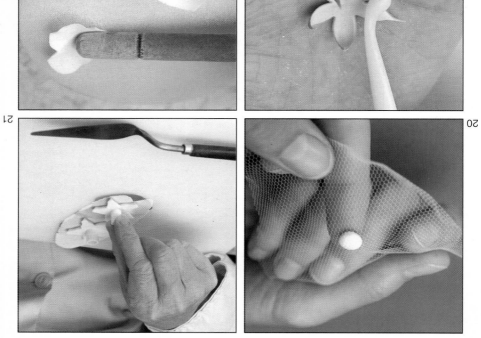

25

How to Make the Wired Rose. *(See Illustration 25)*

1. Make a small hook on the end of a piece of 26 gauge wire and fit a small cone of coloured flowerpaste onto it with rose water, egg white or Gum Arabic glue. The cone should not be longer than the size of the petal to be used — R3. (See illustration 26). Leave to dry.
   N.B. Push the wire into a block of polystyrene for support or you can make a very effective flowerholder by pushing holes into the polystyrene with a paintbrush handle and then insert short pieces of drinking straw.
2. Roll out some coloured flowerpaste very thinly and cut out 2 petals with cutter R3. Thin the edges slightly with the balling tool.
3. Apply a little glue to the first petal and fold right round the cone so that the centre cannot be seen.
4. Apply a little glue to the second petal and fold it opposite the first with its centre over the join of the first petal. Tip the top away from the centre and bend it back slightly. (See illustration 27).
5. Cut out 3 more R3 petals, thin the edges and cup them slightly with the balling tool, keeping the prepared petals covered to stop them drying out too soon. Put a little glue on the side edge of the third petal and wrap round a little higher using the join of the second petal as a guide for the centre of the third petal leaving the unglued side open. Put a little glue on the open side of the third petal and on one side of the fourth petal. Tuck the edge of that petal inside the third and continue in the same way with the fifth petal so that the last three petals interlock. (See illustration 28).

8. When dry, if required, dust the edges of the petals with a contrasting colour petal dust.

7. Add a calyx (R12), made as shown for the briar rose (Step 2), by placing a little glue in the centre of the white side of the calyx and threading onto the stem and pressing gently onto the underside of the petals. Put a small 'golf tee' of green flowerpaste underneath for the hip and mark with a knife. (See illustration 29).

6. Cut out 4 or 5 more petals and place these in the same fashion round the last three but slightly lower and bending the top edges out slightly. More petals can be added if desired.

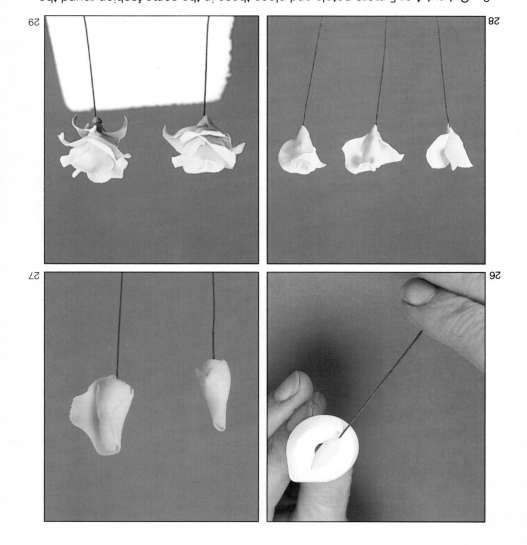

30

(Rose by Maria Sparling)

How to Make the Full Rose. *(See Illustration 30)*

1. Roll out some green paste thinly and cut out a large calyx (R11). Place this in a greased apple tray. (See illustration 31).
2. Roll out some coloured paste very thinly — until you can see through it — and then cut out 5-R1 petals. Dust your hands with cornflour and pick up one petal with your angled spatula, covering the remaining petals with plastic or the lid of your box.
   Place the petal on your hand and smooth and frill out the edge all the way round with the balling tool (OP1) keeping the end of the tool half on the petal and half on your hand. (See illustration 11). Practice makes perfect! Treat the other petal similarly. Do not let them dry out. Using a little rose water, egg white or Gum Arabic glue, place them immediately onto the calyx, each sepal supporting a petal and tucking the edge of each petal under its neighbour thus interlocking them.
3. Repeat with a second layer of 5-R1 petals centring each petal over the joins of the petals in the first layer. Support the outer edges of these petals with small pieces of sponge or paper tissue.
4. Cut out 5-R2 petals, cup them on soft foam and glue them into position as a third layer in the same way, interlocking them as you go.
5. Form a cone of flowerpaste onto the end of a cocktail stick. (See illustration 32). The cone should not be longer than the size of the next petal to be used — R3. (See illustration 26).
6. Cut out 4-R3 petals, apply 'glue' to one side of one of the petals and wrap it round the cone **sideways** to cover the cone.
   Apply the next petal in the same way covering the join of the first one but leaving one edge open.
7. 'Glue' the centre of the third petal and apply it point downwards tucking one edge under the second petal.
8. 'Glue' the fourth petal opposite the third and bend the tops out slightly.

9. Now cut off the bottom of the rose bud you have just made about $^1/_3$rd of the way up, remove it from the cocktail stick and 'glue' it into the centre of the open rose you made in Step 4.

10. Adjust all the petals as required while they are still soft using small pieces of foam for support if required. Leave to dry.

11. Colouring. The petals can be left plain and the 'rose bud' petals can be of a darker shade, or they can be dusted with petal dust when dry.

12. Make leaves as required following the directions on Page 6 and, when dry, colour them with brown and/or darker green petal dust. They may be glazed with confectioners glaze or Gum Arabic glaze. (see recipe page 31).

32

31

33

How to Make the Poppy. (See Illustration 33)

1. Roll out some red flowerpaste very thinly and cut out 4 petals (R2). Thin the edge of a petal with the balling tool and then ball up the centre, pressing outwards, to make the petal wider. Treat each petal similarly. (See illustration 34).

2. Place one petal in a dusted apple tray, put a touch of rose water, egg white or Gum Arabic glue on the point of the petal and place the second petal opposite the first. (See illustration 35).

3. Place the third and fourth petals in the spaces between the first two fixing with a touch of glue on the points. (See illustration 36).

4. To make the centre, roll out a small cone of black paste and insert small black stamens round the cone in the side near the top. (See illustration 37). Make a small round ball of black paste, flatten, and mark about 4 straight lines across the top with a sharp knife. (See illustration 38). Glue this to the top of the cone. Put the complete centre into the middle of the poppy with a little glue.

5. When dry, dust the inside of the poppy near the centre with green petal dust.

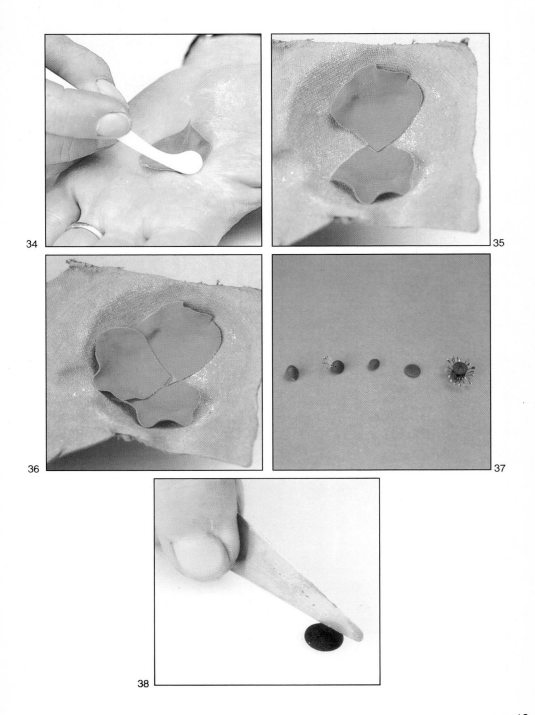

39

How to Make the Buttercup. *(See Illustration 39).*

1. Roll out some yellow flowerpaste very thinly and cut out 5 small petals (R4). Soften the edges and cup slightly on dusted foam with the balling tool. Leave to dry. (See illustration 40).
2. Place a bulb of Royal Icing on a small piece of waxed paper and place the point of each petal into the icing, (see illustration 41), arranging them in a tight circle slightly overlapping and cup shaped. Support in a plastic container, or plastic ring about $\frac{3}{4}''$ dia. (15mm), or a bottle top. (See illustration 42). Leave to dry.
3. Place blob of yellow icing in the centre of the flower and pop in about 10 or 12 yellow stamens.
4. The leaves can be piped or made from green flowerpaste shaped into a small tapered sausage, flattened and marked with a leaf mould.

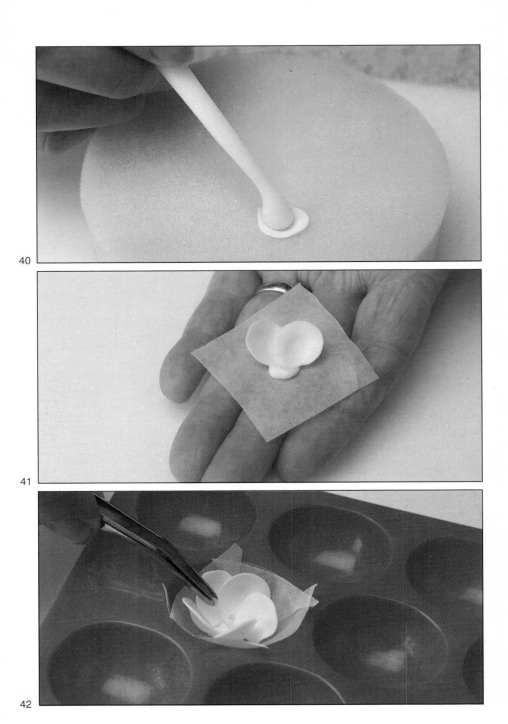

40

41

42

43

How to Make the Sweet Pea. *(See Illustration 43)*

1. Use any colour except yellow. Form a small hook on the end of a piece of 28 gauge wire and cover with a small piece of paste using rose water, egg white or Gum Arabic glue to stick.
2. Roll out some flowerpaste thinly and cut out 1 small rose petal (R3). Smooth the edge with the balling tool, cover thinly with the glue and lay the padded end of the wire onto the petal with the wire along the centre of the petal point downwards. Fold gently round the padded centre, making a neat edge, into a 'cornish pastie' shape. (See illustration 44). Tip back the petal to give it a slight curve. Leave to dry.
3. Roll out some flowerpaste very thinly and cut out 1 rose petal (R2) and 1 briar Rose petal (R14). Flute the briar rose petal with a cocktail stick, (see illustration 45), and glue onto the back of the 'cornish pastie'. Wrap round leaving a gap, and set the wire forward a little. (See illustration 44).
4. Flute the R2 petal with a cocktail stick and glue to the back of the previous petal. Curve back slightly. (See illustration 46).
5. The calyx is made from a tiny 'golf tee' of green paste cut into a star shape with a knife or a tiny star cutter. Make an indentation in the centre of the calyx with a cocktail stick, apply a touch of glue and gently thread the wire through the centre, nestling the flower into the cupped calyx. (See illustration 47).
6. For the tendril, wrap the end of a piece of very thin florists tape round the stem just below the flower and, holding a thin cocktail stick at right-angles to the stem, twist the tape round the stick until you have formed a neat tendril. Gently pull out the cocktail stick. (See illustration 48)

44

45

46

47

48

49

How to Make the Marzipan Rose. *(See Illustrations 49 & 50)*

1. Form a cone of coloured marzipan and then indent right round about ⅓rd of the way up with the outside of your little finger to form a small cone standing on a base. (See illustration 51).
2. Roll out some coloured marzipan very thinly. You will need the non-stick board and rolling pin for this*. Cut out 2 small rose petals (R4), cup them with the balling tool in your sugared hand and fix the first one onto the cone, point down, wrapping it round the cone. Wrap the second petal round the cone opposite to and overlapping the first petal. Curl back slightly. Make sure the cone stays plump.
3. Cut out 3 — larger petals (R3), cup them as before, curl back the edges and fit them round the first two so that they overlap each other. Open out the tops slightly.
4. Cut out 4 — larger petals (R2), cup them slightly more than the previous petals and give them a more pronounced curl back. Fit them slightly lower round the R3 petals. They should tend to fall away slightly from the rose.
5. Remove the base by rolling between the outsides of your little fingers.
* **N.B.** You will notice that no 'glue' has been mentioned. This is because the non-stick board does not need to be dusted and therefore, without the sugar, the marzipan pieces will stick to each other quite naturally.
6. Leaves are made from marzipan using the method shown on Page 6.

24

50

51

25

52

How to Make the Fantasy Flower. *(See Illustration 52)*

1. Make a 'golf tee' of white or coloured flowerpaste, thin out the fat end by rolling with a plastic knitting needle. (See illustration 53). Pop a calyx cutter (R11, R12 or R13) over the stem and cut out the petals. (See illustration 54).
2. Bell the back of the petals outwards with the balling tool in your dusted hand, or bell the opposite way to make a different flower. (See illustration 55).
3. Insert the dry end of a piece of fine wire, moistened at one end, into the centre of the flower pulling it through gently until the moistened end is embedded in the flower. Then bend the wire over just below the point of the tee.
4. Gently push 4 short and 1 long stamen into the centre of the flower with tweezers. Roll out the back of the flower thinly between your finger and thumb. Leave to dry.
5. Dust the edges of the petals with petal dust and put on spots of contrasting colour with an edible pen. Dust the base of the flower with a touch of green petal dust.

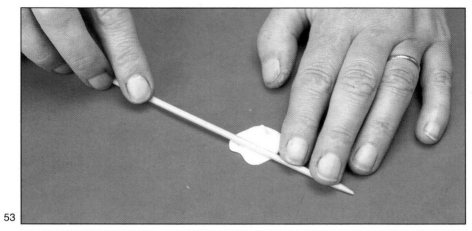

53

54

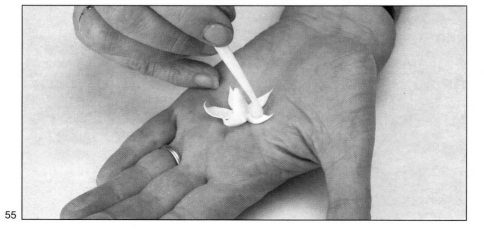

55

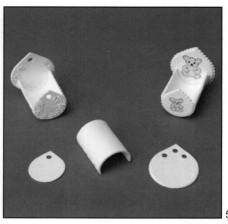

56
57

How to Make the Crib. *(See Illustration 56)*

1. Roll out white flowerpaste or pastillage to medium thickness (about 2mm) and cut out 1 — large rose petal (R1), 1 — medium size (R2) and a rectangle 2″ × 1½″(50×38mm). Decorate them by cutting out very small holes round the edges with a bullet case or blossom cutter, or use Broderie Anglaise.
2. Shape the rectangle over a 1″ dia. (25mm) former and leave all items to dry. (See illustration 57).
3. If required, when dry, a painted decoration may be used on the petals.
4. Fit the two ends and the body together with piped stiff Royal Icing and decorate as required with small flowers, piped motifs and/or ribbons.

How to Make the Plaque. *(See Illustration 56)*

1. Roll out sugarpaste or pastillage fairly thickly and, using the **base** of the Rose Set box as a cutter, cut out a petal-shaped plaque.
2. This can be decorated in various ways — using crimpers round the edge, piping Royal Icing motifs, using Broderie Anglaise, ribbon insertion, painting a picture in the centre, using brush embroidery, bas relief etc. Care is required to only work on the plaque when it is at the appropriate state of dryness to suit the technique being used.

58

59

How to Make the Bedhead. *(See Illustration 58)*

1. Roll out sugarpaste or pastillage fairly thickly and, using the **base** of the Rose Set box as a cutter, cut out a petal-shaped plaque. The whole plaque can be used for the head of the bed, and the foot can be made by cutting off about $\frac{1}{3}$rd of another plaque.
2. Decorate by embossing with a butter pat, embossed handcream bottle top, large buttons, or leather embossing tools. When dry, a delicate effect is created by colouring with petal dust and then gently wiping off some of the powder on the highlights with a damp cloth.
3. Attach to the bed with a little Royal Icing or melted chocolate. (See illustration 59).

60

How to Make the Chocolate Box. *(See illustration 60)*

1. Polish the inside of the Rose Set box and lid with soft tissue or cotton wool.
2. Using a good quality bakers chocolate, melt about 2lbs (900g) in a double saucepan, or in a microwave oven (preferably fitted with a temperature probe) — do not exceed 43°C (110°F). If using a probe melt the chocolate first for about 1½ minutes **without** the probe and then insert the probe into the melted chocolate. It can then be kept automatically at 40°C for as long as you choose.
3. Pour the chocolate into both halves of the box and fill them right up level with the top. Leave to cool until a thick ridge (approx. ⅜″ or 10mm) forms round the edge. Pour out the surplus chocolate, smooth off the edge with a sharp knife where you have poured the chocolate and then place in a refrigerator (**not** freezer) for 2-3 minutes to assist in extracting the chocolate by rapid contraction. When it is ready the chocolate should give an audible 'click'. Put your fingers under the ridge on each side and the chocolate should lift out quite easily.
4. The gloss on the finished items will probably be quite satisfactory for most purposes as it is, but both items can be glazed with a confectioners glaze if required. Pop a sugar flower on top with a little melted chocolate and you will have a splendid gift for any time of the year but particularly at Easter or Christmas.

RECIPES

1. **Flowerpaste A.** 250 grams (½lb) Craigmillars 'Pastello' or Bakels 'Pettinice' **only**. 1 teaspoon Gum Tragacanth.

   Rub 'Trex' on your hands and knead paste until elastic. Wrap tightly in plastic and store in an airtight container. Leave for 24 hours. There is no need to refrigerate. This paste keeps well if worked through say, once a week. Always keep tightly wrapped.

2. **Flowerpaste B.** 250 grams (½lb) sifted icing sugar
   2 scant teaspoons gelatine
   30ml (1oz) water
   1 rounded teaspoon liquid glucose

   Dissolve the gelatine by putting the water in a cup and sprinkling on the gelatine. Stand the cup in a pan of hot water and leave until the gelatine is completely dissolved. When dissolved add the glucose. The liquid should be quite clear before adding it to the icing sugar. Make a well in the icing sugar and stir in the liquid with a knife. Store the paste in a plastic bag and then in an airtight container at room temperature. Leave to stand for 3 or 4 hours before using.

3. **Gum Arabic Glaze.** 60 grams (2ozs) gum arabic powder. (This is sometimes called gum acacia).
   150ml (¼pt) water

   Mix and melt the powder and water in a double boiler. Strain and keep in a refrigerator.
   The solution will keep for months, but sometimes mould appears on the surface. This is harmless and can be removed easily. A few drops of brandy can be added to the solution to prevent this mould from forming.
   'Confectioners glaze' is a better medium if your local retailer stocks it.

4. Gum Arabic Glue. Use proportions of 3:1 of tepid water and Gum Arabic. i.e. 3 teaspoons of water to 1 teaspoon of Gum Arabic. Place in a clean nail varnish container or similar and shake well.

5. Pastillage. 500 grams icing sugar
10 grams gelatine
30 grams Royal Icing
30 grams cornflour
60 grams water

Dissolve the gelatine by putting the water in a cup and sprinkling on the gelatine. Stand the cup in a pan of hot water and leave until the gelatine is completely dissolved. Make a well in the sifted icing sugar and cornflour and stir in the dissolved gelatine with a knife. Mix in the Royal Icing, wrap in clingfilm and store in an airtight container.

6. Royal Icing 450 grams (1lb) icing sugar
* 10 grams (4 × 5ml teaspoons) Albumen (dried hen egg whites) or approx. 3 egg whites
90ml (3 fluid ozs) tepid water

Add Albumen to water and whisk with a wire whisk. Allow to stand for 15 minutes. Re-whisk, place in mixing bowl and gradually add the icing sugar. Mix with a wooden spoon until the consistency of unwhipped cream. Stir at this stage and continue adding the sugar and stirring until the desired consistency is obtained (cold meringue). If using a machine, do not overbeat. Use a 'K' beater on the **lowest** speed.
To test. lift the icing with a spatula and it should be just capable of forming a peak and holding its shape on withdrawing the spatula slowly from the bowl. Scrape down the sides of the bowl and cover with a damp cloth or cling film. Otherwise a crust will form making the icing difficult to use.

* or in accordance with the manufacturers instructions, which may vary slightly from this recipe.